Welcome to the Great Dictionary!

Ah, Canada! Land of maple syrup, ice hockey, and the eternal quest for the perfect toque. But wait—what's that? You're feeling a bit lost in the snowy wilderness of Canadian vernacular? Fear not, brave explorer! You've just stumbled upon the ultimate guide to deciphering our charmingly quirky, often baffling, and occasionally downright baffling Canadian slang.

Ever wondered why Canadians say "eh" at the end of every sentence? Or why "double-double" has nothing to do with gym workouts and everything to do with coffee? It's all here! From "aboot" to "zamboni," this dictionary will be your trusty map through the frosty tundra of our lingo.

So grab your favorite Tim Hortons coffee, slip into your coziest pair of plaid flannel pajamas, and get ready to laugh, learn, and possibly wonder if we've all gone a bit loopy from too much poutine. Welcome to the whimsical world of Canadian slang—where every word is a winter wonderland of its own!

Where is your next travel ?

SCAN THE QR

Get the Slang Dictionary Collection

Slang Dictionaries Availables:

- French
- Mexican
- German
- Italian
- Colombian
- Many More...

TABLE OF CONTENT

A *5*
B *8*
C *11*
D *14*
E *17*
F *20*
G *23*
H *26*
I *30*
J *34*
K *37*
L *41*
M *45*
N *49*
O *52*
P *55*
Q *59*
R *63*
S *67*
T *71*
U *75*
V *79*

W *81*
Y *85*
Z *89*

A

Aboot - Pronounced version of "about".
"What's this all aboot?"
Translation: "What's this all about?"

All-dressed - A flavor of potato chips with a mix of flavors.
"I bought some all-dressed chips for the party."
Translation: "I bought some mixed-flavor chips for the party."

Arse - Canadian variation of "ass."
"Get your arse over here."
Translation: "Get your ass over here."

Arctic front - A cold wave from the north.
"The Arctic front is bringing snow early this year."
Translation: "The cold wave from the north is bringing snow early this year."

As Canadian as possible under the circumstances - A phrase used when you're doing something with a Canadian flavor.
"I'll eat poutine—being as Canadian as possible under the circumstances."
Translation: "I'll eat poutine—keeping it as Canadian as possible."

As crooked as a dog's hind leg - Dishonest or corrupt.
"That politician is as crooked as a dog's hind leg."
Translation: "That politician is very dishonest."

As mad as a meat axe - Extremely angry or crazy.

"He was as mad as a meat axe when he found out."
Translation: "He was extremely angry when he found out."

At the drop of a hat - Immediately or without hesitation.
"He'd help you out at the drop of a hat."
Translation: "He would help you immediately."

At par - On equal footing, especially regarding the U.S. dollar.
"Our dollar is finally at par with the U.S."
Translation: "Our currency is finally equal to the U.S. dollar."

Aurora borealis - The Northern Lights, commonly seen in northern Canada.
"We went up north to see the aurora borealis."
Translation: "We traveled north to see the Northern Lights."

Avro Arrow - A symbol of Canadian engineering excellence, referring to a canceled military jet project.
"The Avro Arrow was ahead of its time."
Translation: "The Avro Arrow was technologically advanced for its era."

Awful sorry - Very apologetic.
"I'm awful sorry about that mistake."
Translation: "I'm very sorry about that mistake."

Aye - A term for agreement, similar to "yes."
"You coming to the game? Aye."
Translation: "Are you coming to the game? Yes."

Aye-aye - A more enthusiastic agreement.
"Need help with the BBQ? Aye-aye!"
Translation: "Need help with the BBQ? Absolutely!"

Auld lang syne - A phrase from a Scottish song meaning "old long since."
"We sang 'Auld Lang Syne' at midnight."
Translation: "We sang 'Auld Lang Syne' at midnight."

Aussie salute - Brushing away flies, especially in summer.
"I keep doing the Aussie salute in this heat."
Translation: "I'm constantly brushing away flies in this heat."

Avro Arrow - A reference to Canadian ingenuity, especially in aviation.
"The Avro Arrow was a marvel of engineering."
Translation: "The Avro Arrow was an engineering marvel."

Attaboy - A term of encouragement or praise.
"You scored the winning goal? Attaboy!"
Translation: "You scored the winning goal? Well done!"

Asphalt jungle - A large, dangerous city.
"Toronto can be an asphalt jungle at times."
Translation: "Toronto can be a rough place at times."

Away with the fairies - Daydreaming or not paying attention.
"She's away with the fairies during class."
Translation: "She's daydreaming during class."

B

Back bacon - A type of cured pork commonly known as Canadian bacon.
"I had a back bacon sandwich for breakfast."
Translation: "I had a Canadian bacon sandwich for breakfast."

Back forty - A remote or undeveloped part of land.
"He's out in the back forty checking the crops."
Translation: "He's out in the remote field checking the crops."

Beauty - Something great or awesome.
"That shot was a beauty!"
Translation: "That shot was amazing!"

Beaver tail - A fried dough pastry often found at fairs.
"Grab a beaver tail before you leave the festival."
Translation: "Get a fried dough pastry before you leave the festival."

Bender - A drinking spree or wild party.
"We went on a bender after the game."
Translation: "We went on a drinking spree after the game."

Biffy - An outdoor toilet, also known as a porta-potty.
"The biffy's just around the corner."
Translation: "The porta-potty is just around the corner."

Blow a gasket - To become very angry.
"Dad blew a gasket when he saw the mess."

Translation: "Dad got really angry when he saw the mess."

Blow the whistle - To expose wrongdoing.
"She blew the whistle on the company's practices."
Translation: "She exposed the company's unethical practices."

Blue line - The line in hockey that marks the offensive zone.
"He crossed the blue line and took a shot."
Translation: "He crossed into the offensive zone and took a shot."

Bogged down - To be stuck or overwhelmed.
"I got bogged down with all the paperwork."
Translation: "I got stuck with all the paperwork."

Boondocks - A remote, rural area.
"We're heading out to the boondocks this weekend."
Translation: "We're heading out to a remote rural area this weekend."

Booze can - An illegal after-hours club.
"We went to a booze can after the bar closed."
Translation: "We went to an illegal club after the bar closed."

Boot - To kick someone out or to expel.
"They booted him out of the bar."
Translation: "They kicked him out of the bar."

Boozer - A heavy drinker.
"He's known as a bit of a boozer in town."

Translation: "He's known as a heavy drinker in town."

Briar - A derogatory term for a French-Canadian.
"He called him a briar, which was really offensive."
Translation: "He insultingly called him a French-Canadian."

Brown out - A partial blackout due to excessive drinking.
"I had a brown out last night; can't remember much."
Translation: "I partially blacked out last night; I can't remember much."

Buds - Friends or buddies.
"We're heading out with the buds tonight."
Translation: "We're going out with our friends tonight."

Bunk - Something that's nonsense or false.
"That excuse is total bunk."
Translation: "That excuse is total nonsense."

Burning the midnight oil - Working late into the night.
"I've been burning the midnight oil to finish this project."
Translation: "I've been working late into the night to finish this project."

Buzz off - Go away or leave.
"Why don't you just buzz off?"
Translation: "Why don't you just go away

C

Canuck - A slang term for a Canadian.
"He's a proud Canuck."
Translation: "He's a proud Canadian."

Capisce - Do you understand?
"You get what I'm saying, capisce?"
Translation: "Do you understand what I'm saying?"

Caribou - Canadian term for reindeer.
"We spotted a caribou during our hike."
Translation: "We saw a reindeer during our hike."

Chesterfield - A couch or sofa.
"Come sit on the chesterfield."
Translation: "Come sit on the couch."

Click - A kilometer.
"We're about 10 clicks away from the town."
Translation: "We're about 10 kilometers away from the town."

Cold enough to freeze the balls off a brass monkey –
Extremely cold.
"It's cold enough to freeze the balls off a brass monkey today."
Translation: "It's extremely cold today."

Cooey - A loud call to attract attention.
"Give a cooey when you're ready."
Translation: "Call out loudly when you're ready."

Cram - To study intensively before an exam.
"I need to cram for my finals."
Translation: "I need to study intensively for my finals."

Crokies - Eyeglass holders that hang around the neck.
"I wear crokies so I don't lose my glasses."
Translation: "I wear eyeglass holders so I don't lose my glasses."

Crown land - Public land owned by the government.
"We camped on crown land last summer."
Translation: "We camped on public land last summer."

Cunning as a shithouse rat - Very clever but in a sneaky way.
"That guy is cunning as a shithouse rat."
Translation: "That guy is very clever but sneaky."

Cut the mustard - To meet expectations or standards.
"I'm not sure he'll cut the mustard in this job."
Translation: "I'm not sure he'll meet the standards in this job."

Cutting it fine - Doing something at the last possible moment.
"You're cutting it fine, aren't you?"
Translation: "You're doing this at the last possible moment, aren't you?"

Coastie - Someone from the east or west coast of Canada.
"He's a true coastie, born and raised."
Translation: "He's a true coastal person, born and raised."

Cottage - A vacation home, often in a rural area.
"We're heading to the cottage this weekend."
Translation: "We're going to our vacation home this weekend."

Cowtown - A nickname for Calgary, Alberta.
"I'm heading to Cowtown for the rodeo."
Translation: "I'm going to Calgary for the rodeo."

Crapshoot - Something unpredictable or risky.
"Investing in that stock is a crapshoot."
Translation: "Investing in that stock is very risky."

Crow's Nest - The upper level of a lookout tower or ship.
"We climbed up to the crow's nest for a better view."
Translation: "We climbed to the upper level of the lookout tower for a better view."

Canadian tuxedo - An outfit consisting of a denim jacket and jeans.
"He showed up in a full Canadian tuxedo."
Translation: "He showed up wearing a denim jacket and jeans."

Curling - A sport involving sliding stones on ice, popular in Canada.
"We're going curling after work."
Translation: "We're going to play curling after work."

D

Dart - A cigarette.
"Let's go for a dart."
Translation: "Let's go for a cigarette."

Double-double - A coffee with two creams and two sugars.
"I'll take a double-double from Tim's."
Translation: "I'll have a coffee with two creams and two sugars from Tim Hortons."

Deke - To fake out an opponent, usually in hockey.
"He deked the goalie and scored!"
Translation: "He faked out the goalie and scored!"

Depot - A Royal Canadian Mounted Police training facility.
"He's heading to depot for training."
Translation: "He's going to the RCMP training facility."

Down East - Refers to the eastern provinces of Canada.
"We're vacationing down east this year."
Translation: "We're vacationing in the eastern provinces of Canada this year."

Ditch - To leave or abandon something or someone.
"Let's ditch this party and go home."
Translation: "Let's leave this party and go home."

Dog's breakfast - A mess or something disorganized.
"That presentation was a dog's breakfast."
Translation: "That presentation was a complete mess."

Doolally - Crazy or insane.
"She's gone completely doolally over that new game."
Translation: "She's gone completely crazy over that new game."

Dozer - A bulldozer or heavy machinery.
"They brought in a dozer to clear the land."
Translation: "They brought in a bulldozer to clear the land."

Drag - A long, boring task or situation.
"Filing all that paperwork is such a drag."
Translation: "Filing all that paperwork is so boring."

Drive-in - An outdoor cinema where people watch movies from their cars.
"We're going to the drive-in tonight."
Translation: "We're going to an outdoor cinema tonight."

Drop the gloves - To start a fight, especially in hockey.
"He dropped the gloves in the first period."
Translation: "He started a fight in the first period."

Dub - A W, meaning a win, especially in sports.
"We got the dub last night!"
Translation: "We won last night!"

Ducks in a row - To get organized or prepared.
"I need to get my ducks in a row before the meeting."
Translation: "I need to get organized before the meeting."

Duddy - An old or worn-out item.
"That sweater is getting a bit duddy."
Translation: "That sweater is getting old and worn out."

Dumb luck - Good luck without effort or skill.
"He won by dumb luck."
Translation: "He won by sheer luck."

Dust-up - A minor fight or argument.
"They had a little dust-up after the game."
Translation: "They had a minor argument after the game."

Duster - A hockey player who rarely plays.
"He's just a duster, sitting on the bench all game."
Translation: "He's a player who rarely plays, sitting on the bench all game."

Dynamite - Something great or excellent.
"That new album is dynamite!"
Translation: "That new album is excellent!"

Dying breed - Something or someone becoming rare or extinct.
"Cowboys are a dying breed in Canada."
Translation: "Cowboys are becoming rare in Canada."

E

Eh - A word added to the end of sentences, often for confirmation.
"It's a nice day, eh?"
Translation: "It's a nice day, right?"

Eavestrough - A rain gutter.
"The eavestrough needs cleaning."
Translation: "The rain gutter needs cleaning."

Eh-hole - A term for an annoying or rude Canadian.
"He's being a real eh-hole today."
Translation: "He's being really annoying today."

End of the road - A situation with no further options.
"This is the end of the road for our team."
Translation: "This is the last option for our team."

Eskimo - An outdated term for the Inuit people.
"Eskimo pies are no longer called that."
Translation: "Inuit pies are no longer called that."

Eh team - A term for Canada's Olympic team.
"The Eh team brought home the gold!"
Translation: "Canada's Olympic team brought home the gold!"

English-Canadian - A Canadian whose first language is English.
"He's an English-Canadian from Ontario."
Translation: "He's a Canadian whose first language is English from Ontario."

Epic - Something amazing or extraordinary.
"That concert was epic!"
Translation: "That concert was amazing!"

Eskimo kiss - Rubbing noses as a form of greeting.
"They exchanged an Eskimo kiss at the airport."
Translation: "They rubbed noses in greeting at the airport."

Even steven - Fair and equal.
"We're even steven now."
Translation: "We're all square now."

Eh to Zed - A phrase meaning everything or the whole alphabet.
"I know the rules from eh to zed."
Translation: "I know all the rules thoroughly."

E-bike - An electric bicycle.
"I bought an e-bike to commute."
Translation: "I bought an electric bicycle to commute."

Elbow grease - Hard work or effort.
"It'll take some elbow grease to clean that up."
Translation: "It'll take a lot of effort to clean that up."

Elk - A large deer native to Canada.
"We saw an elk on our hike."
Translation: "We saw a large deer on our hike."

Eh? - Used to express surprise or disbelief.
"She won the lottery, eh?"
Translation: "She won the lottery, really?"

Eye candy - Something or someone pleasing to look at.
"That new car is pure eye candy."
Translation: "That new car is very pleasing to look at."

Eh, buddy? - A friendly greeting or way to get attention.
"How's it going, eh, buddy?"
Translation: "How are you, friend?"

Euchre - A card game popular in Canada.
"We played euchre all night."
Translation: "We played a card game all night."

F

Frosh - A first-year student at university.
"The frosh are all moving into residence today."
Translation: "The first-year students are all moving into the dorms today."

Fubar - Completely messed up or broken.
"This project is totally fubar."
Translation: "This project is completely messed up."

Fire up the barbie - Start the barbecue.
"Let's fire up the barbie for dinner."
Translation: "Let's start the barbecue for dinner."

Flat out like a lizard drinking - Very busy.
"I've been flat out like a lizard drinking all week."
Translation: "I've been extremely busy all week."

Fogged in - Unable to travel due to fog.
"We're fogged in at the airport."
Translation: "We're stuck at the airport because of the fog."

Fossil - An older person or something outdated.
"That computer is a fossil."
Translation: "That computer is outdated."

French Canadian - A Canadian whose first language is French.
"She's a French Canadian from Quebec."
Translation: "She's a Canadian whose first language is French from Quebec."

Frigid - Extremely cold.
"It's frigid out there today."
Translation: "It's extremely cold outside today."

Fuddle-duddle - A polite way of saying "f*** off."
"He told them to fuddle-duddle."
Translation: "He told them to politely go away."

Full Mountie - Dressed in the formal uniform of the Royal Canadian Mounted Police.
"He was in full Mountie for the parade."
Translation: "He was fully dressed in the formal RCMP uniform for the parade."

Forty below - Extremely cold weather, around -40°C.
"It's forty below with the windchill today."
Translation: "It's extremely cold today with the windchill."

Frostback - A Canadian who moves to the United States.
"He's a frostback living in Florida now."
Translation: "He's a Canadian living in Florida now."

Fuddle - A state of confusion or intoxication.
"He was in a bit of a fuddle after all those drinks."
Translation: "He was quite confused after all those drinks."

Furnace room - A basement room where the heating system is located.
"Check the furnace room for that noise."
Translation: "Check the basement room with the heating system for that noise."

Flannel - A warm, plaid shirt commonly worn in Canada.
"I bought a new flannel for the winter."
Translation: "I bought a new plaid shirt for the winter."

Flick - A movie.
"Let's go see a flick tonight."
Translation: "Let's go see a movie tonight."

Flyer - A promotional leaflet or advertisement.
"Check the flyer for grocery deals."
Translation: "Check the promotional leaflet for grocery deals."

Fluke - Something that happens by chance or accident.
"Winning that game was a fluke."
Translation: "Winning that game was purely by chance."

French fry guy - A person who only eats junk food.
"He's a real French fry guy, never eats healthy."
Translation: "He always eats junk food and never eats healthy."

Fuddy-duddy - An old-fashioned person.
"My grandpa's a bit of a fuddy-duddy."
Translation: "My grandpa is a bit old-fashioned."

G

Goon - An enforcer or tough guy in hockey.
"He's the team's goon, always ready to fight."
Translation: "He's the team's enforcer, always ready to fight."

Gitch - Men's underwear.
"I need to do laundry, I'm out of gitch."
Translation: "I need to do laundry; I'm out of underwear."

Gravy train - A situation where someone makes easy money.
"He's riding the gravy train with that cushy job."
Translation: "He's making easy money with that comfortable job."

Grind - To work hard at something.
"I've been grinding all week to meet the deadline."
Translation: "I've been working hard all week to meet the deadline."

Grok - To understand something deeply.
"It took me a while to grok the new system."
Translation: "It took me a while to fully understand the new system."

Grub - Food.
"Let's grab some grub after the game."
Translation: "Let's get some food after the game."

Gunt - A slang term for the belly area, a mix of gut and another word.

"He's got a bit of a gunt."
Translation: "He's got a bit of a belly."

Gas bar - A gas station.
"Stop at the gas bar for some snacks."
Translation: "Stop at the gas station for some snacks."

Gore - A triangular piece of land between two roads.
"There's a little park on the gore by my house."
Translation: "There's a small park in the triangular area between two roads near my house."

Gong show - A chaotic or poorly managed event.
"That meeting was a total gong show."
Translation: "That meeting was chaotic and poorly managed."

Grizzly - A large bear found in Canada.
"We saw a grizzly on our camping trip."
Translation: "We saw a large bear on our camping trip."

Get on the wrong side of - To annoy or anger someone.
"You don't want to get on the wrong side of her."
Translation: "You don't want to annoy her."

Goin' out for a rip - Going for a fun ride or drive.
"We're goin' out for a rip in the truck."
Translation: "We're going for a fun drive in the truck."

Green bin - A bin for compost or organic waste.
"Put the food scraps in the green bin."
Translation: "Put the food scraps in the compost bin."

Grits - Members of the Liberal Party of Canada.
"The Grits won the election this year."
Translation: "The Liberal Party won the election this year."

Give'r - To put in a lot of effort or go all out.
"Just give'r and you'll finish the race!"
Translation: "Give it your all and you'll finish the race!"

Gordie Howe hat trick - In hockey, when a player scores a goal, gets an assist, and gets in a fight in the same game.
"He got a Gordie Howe hat trick last night!"
Translation: "He scored a goal, got an assist, and got in a fight in the same game last night!"

Gitchy - Something tacky or in bad taste.
"That sweater is a bit gitchy, don't you think?"
Translation: "That sweater is a bit tacky, don't you think?"

Graveyard shift - A work shift that takes place late at night.
"I'm on the graveyard shift this week."
Translation: "I'm working late at night this week."

Grow-op - An illegal operation where marijuana is grown.
"The police busted a grow-op in the neighborhood."
Translation: "The police shut down an illegal marijuana-growing operation in the neighborhood."

H

Habs - Short for "Les Habitants," a nickname for the Montreal Canadiens hockey team.
"The Habs are playing tonight."
Translation: "The Montreal Canadiens are playing tonight."

Hoser - A derogatory term for an unsophisticated or uneducated Canadian.
"Don't be such a hoser!"
Translation: "Don't be so unsophisticated!"

Hang a Larry - To turn left.
"Hang a Larry at the next intersection."
Translation: "Turn left at the next intersection."

Hang a Roger - To turn right.
"Hang a Roger after the light."
Translation: "Turn right after the light."

Hoserama - A fun or exciting event.
"That party was a total hoserama!"
Translation: "That party was a lot of fun!"

Hoof it - To walk or run.
"We had to hoof it to the bus stop."
Translation: "We had to walk quickly to the bus stop."

Home and native land - A reference to the Canadian national anthem, "O Canada."
"We sang 'home and native land' at the game."
Translation: "We sang the Canadian national anthem at the game."

Hicktown - A small, rural, or unimportant town.
"I grew up in a hicktown, but I love it."
Translation: "I grew up in a small town, but I love it."

Hogtown - A nickname for Toronto, Ontario.
"Hogtown is bustling with tourists this summer."
Translation: "Toronto is bustling with tourists this summer."

Hockey Night in Canada - A popular Canadian TV program that broadcasts hockey games.
"We watched Hockey Night in Canada with the family."
Translation: "We watched the Canadian hockey game broadcast with the family."

Head north - To go north or move to a more rural area.
"We're going to head north for the weekend."
Translation: "We're going to travel to a more rural area for the weekend."

Hoser hose - A large, unwieldy hose used by Canadian firefighters.
"They rolled out the hoser hose to fight the fire."
Translation: "They used a large hose to fight the fire."

Heritage moment - A reference to a famous Canadian historical event or person.
"That was a real heritage moment for Canada."
Translation: "That was a significant historical event for Canada."

Hitchhike - To travel by getting free rides from passing vehicles.

"We used to hitchhike across the country in the summer."
Translation: "We used to get free rides from passing vehicles across the country in the summer."

Hosser - A slang term for someone who is strong or muscular.
"He's a real hosser, always in the gym."
Translation: "He's very strong and always in the gym."

Hoser dance - A silly or goofy dance often done at Canadian parties.
"They started doing the hoser dance at the wedding."
Translation: "They started doing a goofy dance at the wedding."

Hustle - To work hard or move quickly.
"You need to hustle if you want to make it on time."
Translation: "You need to move quickly if you want to make it on time."

Honk - To vomit.
"He honked after too many drinks."
Translation: "He vomited after too many drinks."

Homebrew - Beer or alcohol made at home.
"They served their own homebrew at the party."
Translation: "They served homemade beer at the party."

Highway of Heroes - A section of Highway 401 in Ontario dedicated to fallen Canadian soldiers.
"We drove down the Highway of Heroes yesterday."

Translation: "We drove on the section of Highway 401 dedicated to fallen soldiers yesterday."

I

Igloo - A snow house built by Inuit people.
"They built an igloo in the backyard for fun."
Translation: "They built a snow house in the backyard for fun."

Inukshuk - A stone landmark used by Indigenous people in Canada.
"There's an Inukshuk by the lake."
Translation: "There's a stone landmark by the lake."

Island time - A relaxed or slow pace of life, often associated with coastal or island living.
"We're on island time up here."
Translation: "We live at a relaxed pace up here."

In the bag - Certain to be successful.
"The game is in the bag, we're winning!"
Translation: "We're certain to win the game!"

Iron ring - A ring worn by Canadian engineers as a symbol of their profession.
"He just got his iron ring from university."
Translation: "He just graduated and received his engineering ring."

In the sticks - Living in a remote or rural area.
"They live way out in the sticks."
Translation: "They live in a very remote area."

Inuit - Indigenous people from the Arctic regions of Canada.
"The Inuit have lived in the north for thousands of years."
Translation: "Indigenous people from the Arctic regions of Canada have lived in the north for thousands of years."

Ice road - A temporary road made of ice, used in northern Canada during the winter.
"We drove on the ice road to the community."
Translation: "We drove on a temporary road made of ice to the community."

Inuksuk - Another spelling for Inukshuk, a stone landmark used by Indigenous people in Canada.
"The Inuksuk was built to guide travelers."
Translation: "The stone landmark was built to guide travelers."

Island hop - To travel between islands.
"We island hopped across the Gulf Islands."
Translation: "We traveled between the Gulf Islands."

Igloolik - An Inuit community in Nunavut, Canada.
"Igloolik is known for its rich cultural heritage."
Translation: "The Inuit community in Nunavut is known for its rich cultural heritage."

It's a keeper - Something worth keeping or holding onto.
"That sweater? It's a keeper."
Translation: "That sweater is worth holding onto."

Ice cap - A layer of ice covering a large area, particularly in the Arctic.
"The ice cap is melting due to climate change."
Translation: "The large layer of ice is melting due to climate change."

In from the cold - To be included or accepted after being excluded.
"They brought him in from the cold after years of estrangement."
Translation: "They included him after years of being excluded."

Icebox - A refrigerator or cold storage area.
"Grab the milk from the icebox."
Translation: "Get the milk from the refrigerator."

It's a scorcher - A very hot day.
"It's a scorcher out there today!"
Translation: "It's very hot outside today!"

In a pickle - In a difficult or tricky situation.
"I'm in a pickle with this project."
Translation: "I'm in a difficult situation with this project."

Ice hockey - A sport played on ice, very popular in Canada.
"We're watching ice hockey tonight."
Translation: "We're watching a sport played on ice tonight."

I'm game - Willing or eager to participate.
"You want to go hiking? I'm game!"
Translation: "Do you want to go hiking? I'm eager to join!"

Inuksuit - Plural of Inukshuk, stone landmarks used by Indigenous people in Canada.
"We saw several Inuksuit on our hike."
Translation: "We saw several stone landmarks on our hike."

J

Jays - A nickname for the Toronto Blue Jays baseball team.
"The Jays are playing the Yankees tonight."
Translation: "The Toronto Blue Jays are playing the Yankees tonight."

Johnny Canuck - A personification of Canada, similar to Uncle Sam for the U.S.
"Johnny Canuck would be proud of our team."
Translation: "Canada would be proud of our team."

Jigging - Fishing by jerking the bait up and down.
"We spent the day jigging for cod."
Translation: "We spent the day fishing by jerking the bait up and down for cod."

Jam buster - A donut filled with jam.
"I'll take a jam buster from Tim's."
Translation: "I'll have a donut filled with jam from Tim Hortons."

Juiced - Excited or enthusiastic.
"He was juiced about the concert."
Translation: "He was excited about the concert."

Jacked - Muscular or very fit.
"He's been working out and is totally jacked."
Translation: "He's been working out and is very muscular."

Jigging - A traditional dance or dance style, often in Newfoundland.

"They were jigging all night at the party."
Translation: "They were dancing traditionally all night at the party."

Jiffy - A very short period of time.
"I'll be back in a jiffy."
Translation: "I'll be back very soon."

Just a sec - A request to wait for a brief moment.
"Just a sec, I'm on the phone."
Translation: "Wait a moment, I'm on the phone."

Jackfish - A type of fish found in Canadian waters, also known as Northern Pike.
"We caught a big jackfish at the lake."
Translation: "We caught a large Northern Pike at the lake."

Jitney - A small bus or minibus used for public transport.
"We took a jitney to the city."
Translation: "We took a small bus to the city."

Jet boat - A boat propelled by a jet of water.
"We went on a jet boat ride through the rapids."
Translation: "We went on a boat ride propelled by a jet of water through the rapids."

Jam session - An informal gathering of musicians to play music together.
"We had a jam session in the garage."
Translation: "We played music together informally in the garage."

Johnny-on-the-spot - Someone who is always ready and available.
"He's a real Johnny-on-the-spot when you need help."
Translation: "He's always ready to help when needed."

Juno Awards - Canadian music awards.
"She won a Juno Award for her new album."
Translation: "She won a Canadian music award for her new album."

Jib - To change direction quickly.
"The boat jibed to avoid the rocks."
Translation: "The boat changed direction quickly to avoid the rocks."

Jackrabbit - To start moving suddenly or quickly.
"The car jackrabbited off the line."
Translation: "The car started moving quickly off the line."

Just about - Nearly or almost.
"We're just about there."
Translation: "We're nearly there."

Jewel of the North - A nickname for the city of Yellowknife, Northwest Territories.
"Yellowknife is known as the Jewel of the North."
Translation: "The city of Yellowknife is known as the Jewel of the North."

Johnny on the roll - Someone who is doing well or on a streak.
"He's Johnny on the roll with all those sales."
Translation: "He's on a winning streak with all those sales."

K

Ketchup chips - A popular flavor of potato chips in Canada.
"I love ketchup chips with my sandwich."
Translation: "I enjoy potato chips flavored with ketchup with my sandwich."

Klick - A kilometer.
"We hiked 10 klicks today."
Translation: "We hiked 10 kilometers today."

Kraft Dinner - A brand of boxed macaroni and cheese, commonly eaten in Canada.
"We had Kraft Dinner for lunch."
Translation: "We had boxed macaroni and cheese for lunch."

Kerfuffle - A commotion or fuss.
"There was a bit of a kerfuffle at the meeting."
Translation: "There was a bit of a commotion at the meeting."

Keener - Someone who is overly eager or enthusiastic, especially in school.
"She's a real keener, always the first to raise her hand."
Translation: "She's very eager, always the first to raise her hand."

Kit and kaboodle - Everything, including all parts.
"We packed up the whole kit and kaboodle for the trip."
Translation: "We packed up everything for the trip."

Karaoke - Singing along to recorded music with lyrics displayed on a screen.
"We did karaoke at the bar last night."
Translation: "We sang along to recorded music with lyrics displayed on a screen at the bar last night."

Knickers - A slang term for underwear.
"I need to buy some new knickers."
Translation: "I need to buy some new underwear."

Kiss the cod - A Newfoundland tradition where newcomers kiss a codfish as a rite of passage.
"I had to kiss the cod when I visited Newfoundland."
Translation: "I participated in the Newfoundland tradition of kissing a codfish when I visited."

King's ransom - A large sum of money.
"That car costs a king's ransom."
Translation: "That car costs a lot of money."

Kick up a fuss - To complain or cause a commotion.
"She kicked up a fuss about the service."
Translation: "She complained about the service."

Keep your stick on the ice - Stay focused and keep working hard, especially in hockey.
"Just keep your stick on the ice, and you'll do fine."
Translation: "Stay focused and keep working hard, and you'll do fine."

Klickety-klack - The sound of something moving quickly, like a train.

"The klickety-klack of the train lulled me to sleep."
Translation: "The sound of the train moving quickly lulled me to sleep."

Kickback - A return of part of a sum paid, often as a bribe.
"He got a kickback for the deal."
Translation: "He received a bribe for the deal."

Krafty - A play on the word "crafty," often used to describe someone who is resourceful.
"She's a krafty shopper, always finding the best deals."
Translation: "She's a resourceful shopper, always finding the best deals."

Kangaroo court - A court that ignores recognized standards of law or justice.
"That meeting was a kangaroo court, nothing fair about it."
Translation: "That meeting was completely unfair."

Knee-high by July - A saying about the height of corn crops by mid-summer.
"The corn is knee-high by July, just like it should be."
Translation: "The corn is growing as expected by mid-summer."

Klutz - A clumsy person.
"I'm such a klutz, I keep dropping everything."
Translation: "I'm very clumsy and keep dropping everything."

Kraft dinner fiend - Someone who loves Kraft Dinner, a popular boxed macaroni and cheese in Canada.

"He's a Kraft Dinner fiend, eats it every day."
Translation: "He loves Kraft Dinner and eats it every day."

Kegger - A party where a keg of beer is served.
"We're having a kegger this weekend."
Translation: "We're having a party with a keg of beer this weekend."

L

Loonie - A Canadian one-dollar coin featuring a loon.
"I found a loonie on the sidewalk."
Translation: "I found a Canadian one-dollar coin on the sidewalk."

Loon - A type of bird found in Canada, also on the loonie coin.
"We saw a loon on the lake."
Translation: "We saw a bird on the lake."

Lumberjack - A person who cuts down trees, often associated with Canadian stereotypes.
"He dresses like a lumberjack with all that flannel."
Translation: "He dresses like a person who cuts down trees with all that flannel."

Lacrosse - A sport that originated with Indigenous peoples in Canada.
"We played lacrosse in gym class."
Translation: "We played a sport that originated with Indigenous peoples in gym class."

LCBO - The Liquor Control Board of Ontario, a government-run liquor store.
"I'm going to the LCBO to pick up some wine."
Translation: "I'm going to the government-run liquor store in Ontario to buy some wine."

Lickety-split - Very quickly.
"We need to get this done lickety-split."
Translation: "We need to get this done very quickly."

Lush - A person who drinks alcohol excessively.
"He's turning into a bit of a lush lately."
Translation: "He's been drinking a lot of alcohol lately."

Land of the Midnight Sun - A nickname for the northern parts of Canada where the sun stays up all day during summer.
"I've always wanted to visit the Land of the Midnight Sun."
Translation: "I've always wanted to visit the northern parts of Canada where the sun stays up all day during summer."

Lick - A quick or efficient job.
"He finished the project in a lick."
Translation: "He finished the project very quickly."

Lake Louise - A famous lake in the Canadian Rockies, known for its beauty.
"We visited Lake Louise on our trip."
Translation: "We visited a famous lake in the Canadian Rockies on our trip."

Lumber - To move in a slow, heavy, and awkward way.
"He lumbered into the room after a long day."
Translation: "He moved slowly and heavily into the room after a long day."

Loonie bin - A slang term for a mental institution.
"They sent him to the loonie bin after the incident."
Translation: "They sent him to a mental institution after the incident."

Lush greenery - Refers to abundant, healthy plant life.

"The park was full of lush greenery."
Translation: "The park was full of abundant, healthy plants."

Lobster boil - A traditional Maritime meal where lobsters are boiled and eaten with butter.
"We had a lobster boil down by the shore."
Translation: "We ate a traditional Maritime meal of boiled lobsters down by the shore."

Lac - The French word for "lake," commonly used in Quebec.
"We spent the weekend at Lac Saint-Jean."
Translation: "We spent the weekend at Lake Saint-Jean."

Loggerhead - A type of sea turtle, but can also mean being in a stubborn dispute.
"They were at loggerheads over the decision."
Translation: "They were in a stubborn dispute over the decision."

Little Italy - A neighborhood in many Canadian cities with a large Italian community.
"We had dinner in Little Italy last night."
Translation: "We had dinner in a neighborhood with a large Italian community last night."

Lock and load - Get ready for action.
"Lock and load, it's time to go."
Translation: "Get ready, it's time to go."

Logjam - A situation in which no progress can be made.

"There's a logjam in the negotiations."
Translation: "No progress is being made in the negotiations."

Leafs - A nickname for the Toronto Maple Leafs hockey team.
"The Leafs are playing the Canadiens tonight."
Translation: "The Toronto Maple Leafs are playing the Montreal Canadiens tonight."

M

Mountie - A member of the Royal Canadian Mounted Police (RCMP).
"A Mountie visited our school for a talk."
Translation: "A member of the Royal Canadian Mounted Police visited our school for a talk."

Molson muscle - A slang term for a beer belly, referencing Molson, a popular Canadian beer.
"He's got quite the Molson muscle now."
Translation: "He has quite the beer belly now."

Mickey - A small bottle of liquor, usually 375 ml.
"I grabbed a mickey for the party."
Translation: "I bought a small bottle of liquor for the party."

Muskoka - A popular cottage country area in Ontario.
"We're heading up to Muskoka this weekend."
Translation: "We're going to the cottage country area in Ontario this weekend."

Maple syrup - A sweet syrup made from the sap of sugar maple trees, iconic to Canada.
"We put maple syrup on our pancakes."
Translation: "We added sweet syrup made from maple trees to our pancakes."

Manitoba blizzard - A severe snowstorm typical of Manitoba's winters.
"We got caught in a Manitoba blizzard on our way home."

Translation: "We were caught in a severe snowstorm typical of Manitoba on our way home."

Molson - A popular Canadian beer brand.
"We had a few Molsons at the barbecue."
Translation: "We drank some Canadian beer at the barbecue."

Mitts - Slang for hands or gloves.
"Keep your mitts off my fries!"
Translation: "Keep your hands off my fries!"

Moose knuckle - The male equivalent of a "camel toe," where pants are too tight.
"That guy's jeans are giving him a serious moose knuckle."
Translation: "That guy's jeans are too tight."

Maple Leaf - A symbol of Canada, often referring to the national flag or the Toronto Maple Leafs hockey team.
"The Maple Leaf flies proudly outside the school."
Translation: "The Canadian flag flies proudly outside the school."

Molson Indy - A former annual auto racing event held in Toronto.
"We watched the Molson Indy last summer."
Translation: "We watched the annual auto racing event in Toronto last summer."

Mickey of rum - A small bottle of rum.
"I brought a mickey of rum for the camping trip."
Translation: "I brought a small bottle of rum for the camping trip."

Maritimer - A person from the Maritime provinces of Canada (Nova Scotia, New Brunswick, Prince Edward Island).
"He's a proud Maritimer, born and raised in Nova Scotia."
Translation: "He's proud of being from the Maritime provinces, born and raised in Nova Scotia."

Mountie Stetson - The distinctive hat worn by the RCMP.
"He put on his Mountie Stetson before the parade."
Translation: "He put on his RCMP hat before the parade."

Mangez la puck - A French Canadian expression meaning to play tough in hockey, literally "eat the puck."
"He's the kind of player who will mangez la puck for the team."
Translation: "He's the kind of player who will play tough for the team."

Moose - A large animal native to Canada, often referenced in Canadian culture.
"We spotted a moose in the woods."
Translation: "We saw a large Canadian animal in the woods."

Moulson Export - A type of beer made by Molson.
"I'll have a Moulson Export, please."
Translation: "I'll have a Molson beer, please."

Montreal smoked meat - A type of smoked beef brisket that is popular in Montreal.
"We had Montreal smoked meat sandwiches for lunch."
Translation: "We ate smoked beef brisket sandwiches for lunch."

Maple Leaf Forever - A patriotic Canadian song.
"They sang 'The Maple Leaf Forever' at the ceremony."
Translation: "They sang a patriotic Canadian song at the ceremony."

Mountie red - The distinctive red uniform worn by the Royal Canadian Mounted Police.
"He looked sharp in his Mountie red at the event."
Translation: "He looked sharp in his RCMP red uniform at the event."

N

Newfie - A colloquial term for a person from Newfoundland, sometimes considered derogatory.
"My friend's a proud Newfie from St. John's."
Translation: "My friend is a proud person from Newfoundland, from St. John's."

Nanaimo bar - A popular Canadian dessert made with layers of chocolate, custard, and coconut.
"She made a batch of Nanaimo bars for the party."
Translation: "She made a Canadian dessert for the party."

Northern lights - The Aurora Borealis, visible in northern parts of Canada.
"We saw the Northern Lights in Yukon."
Translation: "We saw the Aurora Borealis in Yukon."

Nunavut - Canada's newest and northernmost territory, home to many Inuit people.
"Nunavut became a territory in 1999."
Translation: "The northernmost territory of Canada became a territory in 1999."

Northerner - A person from the northern part of Canada.
"He's a tough Northerner, used to the cold."
Translation: "He's a person from northern Canada, used to the cold."

Nipply - Slang for cold weather that makes your nipples stand up.
"It's a bit nipply outside today."
Translation: "It's quite cold outside today."

Nose to the grindstone - To work hard and diligently.
"She's got her nose to the grindstone studying for exams."
Translation: "She's working hard studying for exams."

Newfie steak - A term for bologna, popular in Newfoundland.
"We had Newfie steak for breakfast."
Translation: "We had bologna for breakfast."

Nickel - A five-cent coin in Canada, often featuring a beaver.
"I found a nickel under the couch."
Translation: "I found a five-cent coin under the couch."

Northern gateway - A term used for cities that are the starting point for exploring Canada's northern regions.
"Edmonton is the northern gateway to the Arctic."
Translation: "Edmonton is the starting point for exploring Canada's northern regions."

Nippy - Chilly or cold weather.
"It's pretty nippy out, better wear a scarf."
Translation: "It's quite chilly outside, better wear a scarf."

Newfie screech - A strong rum from Newfoundland, often used in the "screech-in" ceremony.
"We took a shot of Newfie screech to celebrate."
Translation: "We drank strong rum from Newfoundland to celebrate."

No-see-um - Tiny, biting insects common in northern Canada.

"The no-see-ums were terrible at the campsite."
Translation: "The tiny biting insects were terrible at the campsite."

Nod - To nap or fall asleep briefly.
"I had a quick nod on the bus."
Translation: "I had a brief nap on the bus."

New Year's Levee - A Canadian tradition of holding open houses on New Year's Day.
"We attended the New Year's Levee at City Hall."
Translation: "We attended the traditional open house at City Hall on New Year's Day."

Nautical miles - A unit of distance used in marine and air navigation, equal to 1.852 kilometers.
"The boat traveled 10 nautical miles down the coast."
Translation: "The boat traveled 10 marine distance units down the coast."

Noddy - A term for a silly or foolish person.
"Don't be such a noddy, read the instructions first."
Translation: "Don't be so foolish, read the instructions first."

O

Oh yeah? - An expression of disbelief or surprise.
"I won the lottery! Oh yeah?"
Translation: "I won the lottery! Really?"

Oot and aboot - A Canadian way of saying "out and about."
"We were oot and aboot in the city."
Translation: "We were out and about in the city."

Ontario - The most populous province in Canada, home to Toronto and Ottawa.
"We took a road trip through Ontario."
Translation: "We took a road trip through the province of Ontario."

Oiler - A nickname for a player from the Edmonton Oilers hockey team.
"The Oilers are playing tonight."
Translation: "The Edmonton Oilers hockey team is playing tonight."

On the rocks - A drink served over ice.
"I'll have a whiskey on the rocks."
Translation: "I'll have whiskey served over ice."

Out east - Refers to the eastern provinces of Canada, particularly the Maritimes.
"I'm heading out east for the summer."
Translation: "I'm going to the eastern provinces of Canada for the summer."

O Canada - The national anthem of Canada.
"Everyone stood up to sing O Canada."
Translation: "Everyone stood up to sing the national anthem."

Off the rails - Going out of control.
"The party went off the rails last night."
Translation: "The party got out of control last night."

Outhouse - An outdoor toilet, commonly found in rural areas.
"We had to use the outhouse at the cabin."
Translation: "We had to use the outdoor toilet at the cabin."

Oh for sure - A Canadian expression meaning "definitely" or "of course."
"Are you coming to the game? Oh for sure!"
Translation: "Are you coming to the game? Definitely!"

On the back burner - To postpone or delay something.
"We've put that project on the back burner for now."
Translation: "We've postponed that project for now."

Okanagan - A region in British Columbia known for its wineries and fruit orchards.
"We toured the Okanagan during our vacation."
Translation: "We visited the region in British Columbia known for wineries and orchards during our vacation."

On the button - Exactly correct or on time.
"He hit the mark right on the button."
Translation: "He was exactly correct or on time."

Orchard - A piece of land planted with fruit trees, common in parts of Canada.
"We visited an apple orchard in the fall."
Translation: "We visited a piece of land planted with apple trees in the fall."

Off the hook - To escape a difficult situation or responsibility.
"He's off the hook for washing dishes tonight."
Translation: "He escaped the responsibility of washing dishes tonight."

On thin ice - In a risky or precarious situation.
"You're on thin ice with the boss."
Translation: "You're in a risky situation with the boss."

Oh fer sure - A stronger affirmation than "Oh yeah," commonly used in rural Canada.
"You going fishing? Oh fer sure!"
Translation: "Are you going fishing? Definitely!"

Out west - Refers to the western provinces of Canada, like British Columbia and Alberta.
"I'm planning a trip out west next year."
Translation: "I'm planning a trip to the western provinces of Canada next year."

Old man winter - A personification of winter weather.
"Old man winter is really hitting hard this year."
Translation: "The winter weather is really severe this year."

P

Poutine - A classic Canadian dish of fries topped with cheese curds and gravy.
"We had poutine at the diner."
Translation: "We ate a dish of fries with cheese curds and gravy at the diner."

Pop - A term for soft drinks, used commonly in Canada.
"I'll grab a pop from the fridge."
Translation: "I'll get a soft drink from the fridge."

Pegger - A nickname for someone from Winnipeg.
"She's a proud Pegger."
Translation: "She's a proud person from Winnipeg."

Parkade - A multi-level parking garage.
"We parked in the downtown parkade."
Translation: "We parked in the multi-level parking garage downtown."

Peg - Another nickname for Winnipeg.
"We're heading to the Peg this weekend."
Translation: "We're going to Winnipeg this weekend."

Polar vortex - A mass of cold air that brings extremely cold temperatures.
"The polar vortex has us all freezing."
Translation: "The mass of cold air is causing extremely cold temperatures."

Pogey - Slang for unemployment benefits.

"He's been on pogey for a few months."
Translation: "He's been receiving unemployment benefits for a few months."

Pogey stick - A type of stick used to poke things, often used in fishing.
"He used a pogey stick to check the ice thickness."
Translation: "He used a stick to check how thick the ice was."

Portage - The practice of carrying a canoe overland between waterways.
"We had to portage our canoe around the rapids."
Translation: "We had to carry our canoe overland around the rapids."

Provinces - The main territorial divisions of Canada.
"Canada is made up of ten provinces and three territories."
Translation: "Canada is divided into ten territorial regions and three territories."

Parka - A heavy winter coat.
"I need to buy a new parka before winter."
Translation: "I need to buy a new heavy winter coat before winter."

Parliament Hill - The seat of Canada's federal government in Ottawa.
"We visited Parliament Hill during our trip to Ottawa."
Translation: "We visited the seat of Canada's federal government during our trip to Ottawa."

Prairies - The flat, expansive regions of Canada's western provinces.
"The prairies stretch for miles."
Translation: "The flat, expansive regions of Canada's western provinces stretch for miles."

Paddle - To use a paddle to propel a canoe or kayak.
"We paddled down the river all afternoon."
Translation: "We used paddles to propel our canoe down the river all afternoon."

Pogey stamps - Slang for food stamps, welfare benefits.
"He had to use pogey stamps to get by."
Translation: "He had to use welfare benefits to get by."

Pancake Bay - A scenic bay in Ontario known for its beaches.
"We spent the day at Pancake Bay."
Translation: "We spent the day at a scenic bay known for its beaches in Ontario."

Parka party - A party held outdoors in winter, with everyone dressed in heavy coats.
"We had a parka party to celebrate the first snow."
Translation: "We had an outdoor party in winter to celebrate the first snow, with everyone wearing heavy coats."

Panorama - A wide, unobstructed view of an area.
"The panorama from the top of the mountain was stunning."
Translation: "The wide, unobstructed view from the top of the mountain was stunning."

Prairie oysters - A dish made from bull testicles, commonly served in Canada's ranching regions.
"They served prairie oysters at the barbecue."
Translation: "They served a dish made from bull testicles at the barbecue."

Pow wow - A traditional Indigenous gathering with dancing, singing, and cultural celebrations.
"We attended a pow wow in the summer."
Translation: "We attended a traditional Indigenous gathering with dancing and singing in the summer."

Q

Québécois - A French-speaking person from Quebec.
"He's a proud Québécois with a deep love for his culture."
Translation: "He's a proud person from Quebec with a deep love for his culture."

Quinte - A region in Ontario known for its bay and scenic views.
"We went fishing in the Bay of Quinte."
Translation: "We went fishing in a scenic bay region in Ontario."

Qallunaat - A term used by Inuit people to refer to non-Inuit, particularly white people.
"The Qallunaat visited our village last week."
Translation: "Non-Inuit people visited our village last week."

Quad - A four-wheeled all-terrain vehicle (ATV).
"We took the quad out for a spin on the trails."
Translation: "We rode the four-wheeled ATV on the trails."

Queen's Park - The location of Ontario's provincial legislature in Toronto.
"They're holding a protest at Queen's Park today."
Translation: "A protest is happening at the location of Ontario's provincial legislature in Toronto today."

Quench - To satisfy thirst.
"That cold water really quenched my thirst."
Translation: "The cold water satisfied my thirst."

Quesnel - A small city in British Columbia, known for its natural beauty.
"We passed through Quesnel on our way to the Rockies."
Translation: "We drove through a small city in British Columbia known for its natural beauty on our way to the Rockies."

Quicksand - A deep, soft area of sand that can engulf people or objects.
"Be careful, there's quicksand near the riverbank."
Translation: "Be careful, there's deep, soft sand that can engulf you near the riverbank."

Quinzhee - A snow shelter built by hollowing out a pile of snow.
"We built a quinzhee to stay warm during the winter camping trip."
Translation: "We built a snow shelter to stay warm during the winter camping trip."

Quiet time - A period of peace and quiet, often observed in Canadian households.
"We have quiet time after dinner every night."
Translation: "We observe a period of peace and quiet after dinner every night."

Queen's Counsel - A title awarded to a lawyer in Canada for exceptional merit.
"She was appointed Queen's Counsel for her outstanding legal work."
Translation: "She was given a title for her exceptional merit as a lawyer."

Quintessentially Canadian - Something that is very typical or representative of Canadian culture.
"Hockey is quintessentially Canadian."
Translation: "Hockey is very typical or representative of Canadian culture."

Quota - A set limit or amount, often used in fishing or hunting regulations.
"We reached our quota for the day."
Translation: "We met the set limit for the day."

Quebec winter - Refers to the long, cold, and snowy winters typical of Quebec.
"We're in for a real Quebec winter this year."
Translation: "We're expecting a long, cold, and snowy winter typical of Quebec this year."

Quarry - A place where stone is dug out of the ground.
"The old quarry has been turned into a park."
Translation: "The place where stone used to be dug out of the ground has been turned into a park."

Quarterback - The player who directs the offense in Canadian football.
"The quarterback led the team to victory."
Translation: "The player directing the offense in football led the team to victory."

Quill - A large feather, or the spine of a porcupine, used in Indigenous art.
"She made beautiful quillwork on the basket."

Translation: "She decorated the basket with beautiful Indigenous art made from large feathers or porcupine spines."

Quaint - An old-fashioned charm, often used to describe small towns or villages.
"We visited a quaint little town on our road trip."
Translation: "We visited a small town with old-fashioned charm on our road trip."

Queso - Spanish for cheese, sometimes used in Canadian cuisine with Latin American influences.
"We added some queso to our nachos."
Translation: "We added some cheese to our nachos."

R

Rink rat - A person who spends a lot of time at the ice rink, often practicing or playing hockey.
"He's a real rink rat, always practicing his slapshot."
Translation: "He's someone who spends a lot of time at the ice rink, always practicing his slapshot."

Rye - Slang for Canadian whisky, often made from rye grain.
"Pour me a glass of rye, will you?"
Translation: "Pour me a glass of Canadian whisky, please."

Ruckus - A noisy commotion or disturbance.
"There was a ruckus outside the bar last night."
Translation: "There was a noisy commotion outside the bar last night."

Rodeo - A western event with contests in cattle roping, bronco riding, and more, common in Canada's prairie provinces.
"We went to the rodeo in Calgary."
Translation: "We attended the western event with contests in Calgary."

RCMP - Abbreviation for the Royal Canadian Mounted Police.
"The RCMP is investigating the incident."
Translation: "The Royal Canadian Mounted Police is investigating the incident."

Ribfest - A festival celebrating barbecued ribs, common in Canadian cities during the summer.

"We had the best ribs at Ribfest."
Translation: "We ate the best barbecued ribs at the festival."

Roughing it - To live in basic, often uncomfortable conditions, typically while camping.
"We're roughing it at the campsite this weekend."
Translation: "We're living in basic conditions at the campsite this weekend."

Rugged - Describes someone or something as tough or sturdy, often used for Canadian wilderness or people.
"He's a rugged outdoorsman."
Translation: "He's a tough outdoorsman."

Raptor - A term often used for the Toronto Raptors basketball team.
"The Raptors won the game last night."
Translation: "The Toronto basketball team won the game last night."

Red and white - Refers to the colors of the Canadian flag.
"I'm wearing red and white for Canada Day."
Translation: "I'm wearing the colors of the Canadian flag for Canada Day."

Rideau - Refers to the Rideau Canal in Ottawa, often used for skating in winter.
"We skated on the Rideau all afternoon."
Translation: "We skated on the canal in Ottawa all afternoon."

Roadie - A drink to go, or a person who travels with a band to help set up.
"Grab a roadie for the drive."
Translation: "Get a drink to go for the drive."

Rockies - The Rocky Mountains, a major mountain range in Canada.
"We went hiking in the Rockies."
Translation: "We went hiking in the Rocky Mountains."

Rez - Short for "reservation," often used to refer to Indigenous communities.
"He grew up on the rez."
Translation: "He grew up on a reservation."

Root for - To support a team or individual in a competition.
"I'm rooting for the Leafs tonight."
Translation: "I'm supporting the Toronto Maple Leafs tonight."

Raven - A large, black bird common in Canada, often associated with Indigenous myths.
"A raven perched on the tree outside."
Translation: "A large black bird perched on the tree outside."

Riding - A Canadian electoral district.
"She's running for office in the northern riding."
Translation: "She's a candidate for office in the northern electoral district."

Rumrunner - A person or ship that smuggled alcohol during Prohibition.
"They found an old rumrunner's shipwreck on the coast."
Translation: "They found a shipwreck of someone who smuggled alcohol during Prohibition on the coast."

Redneck - A derogatory term for a rural person, often with conservative views.
"He's just a redneck with a big truck."
Translation: "He's just a rural person with a big truck."

Rockhound - A person who collects or hunts for rocks, minerals, and fossils.
"She's a passionate rockhound, always looking for new finds."

S

Skookum - A term from British Columbia meaning strong, reliable, or impressive.
"That's a skookum idea!"
Translation: "That's a strong and impressive idea!"

Sook - A slang term for someone who is whining or acting cowardly.
"Don't be such a sook!"
Translation: "Don't be such a whiner!"

Snowbird - A Canadian who spends the winter in a warmer climate, often in the southern U.S.
"My grandparents are snowbirds in Florida."
Translation: "My grandparents spend the winter in Florida."

Spud - A potato, often used in reference to those grown in Prince Edward Island.
"We're having PEI spuds for dinner."
Translation: "We're having potatoes from Prince Edward Island for dinner."

Slapshot - A powerful shot in hockey where the stick is swung forcefully.
"He scored with a wicked slapshot."
Translation: "He scored with a powerful shot in hockey."

Screech-in - A Newfoundland tradition where visitors drink a shot of screech (rum) and kiss a cod.

"They made me do a screech-in on my first visit to Newfoundland."
Translation: "They made me take part in a Newfoundland tradition involving drinking rum and kissing a cod."

Shag - A Newfoundland term for a party, often with live music.
"We went to a great shag last night."
Translation: "We went to a great party with live music last night."

Supper - The evening meal, commonly used in rural areas of Canada.
"What's for supper tonight?"
Translation: "What's for dinner tonight?"

Stag and doe - A pre-wedding party held to raise money for the bride and groom.
"We're going to their stag and doe this weekend."
Translation: "We're attending their pre-wedding fundraising party this weekend."

Sunblock - A term for sunscreen, especially needed during Canadian summers
"Don't forget your sunblock at the beach."
Translation: "Don't forget your sunscreen at the beach."

Skidoo - A snowmobile, often used in winter sports or travel in Canada.
"We went skidooing all weekend."
Translation: "We rode snowmobiles all weekend."

Schnook - A foolish person or someone easily taken advantage of.
"Don't be a schnook, stand up for yourself."
Translation: "Don't be a fool, stand up for yourself."

Suds - Slang for beer.
"We grabbed some suds and watched the game."
Translation: "We got some beer and watched the game."

Squarehead - A derogatory term for a stubborn or dull person, historically used for Germans or Scandinavians.
"He's such a squarehead about it."
Translation: "He's being so stubborn about it."

Sundog - A natural phenomenon where bright spots appear on either side of the sun, often seen in cold Canadian winters.
"We saw a beautiful sundog this morning."
Translation: "We saw bright spots on either side of the sun this morning."

Shindig - A lively party or gathering.
"We're throwing a shindig for Canada Day."
Translation: "We're having a lively party for Canada Day."

Scallywag - A playful term for a mischievous person.
"That little scallywag stole my hat!"
Translation: "That mischievous person stole my hat!"

Sook and peck - An affectionate term for a quick kiss.
"Give me a sook and peck before you go."
Translation: "Give me a quick kiss before you go."

Sore loser - Someone who doesn't handle losing well.
"Don't be a sore loser, it's just a game."
Translation: "Don't be upset about losing, it's just a game."

T

Toque - A knit cap worn in winter.
"Don't forget your toque, it's freezing outside."
Translation: "Don't forget your knit cap, it's freezing outside."

Timbit - A bite-sized doughnut hole from Tim Hortons, a popular Canadian coffee chain.
"I grabbed a box of Timbits for the office."
Translation: "I bought a box of doughnut holes for the office."

Timmies - A common nickname for Tim Hortons.
"Let's meet at Timmies for coffee."
Translation: "Let's meet at Tim Hortons for coffee."

Tundra - The vast, treeless Arctic regions in Canada.
"The tundra is beautiful in its own way."
Translation: "The vast, treeless Arctic region is beautiful in its own way."

Toonie - A two-dollar Canadian coin.
"I found a toonie on the sidewalk."
Translation: "I found a two-dollar coin on the sidewalk."

Timmy's run - A quick trip to Tim Hortons for coffee or snacks.
"I'm doing a Timmy's run, want anything?"
Translation: "I'm making a quick trip to Tim Hortons, do you want anything?"

Trucker hat - A type of baseball cap with a mesh back, popular in rural areas.
"He always wears a trucker hat."
Translation: "He always wears a baseball cap with a mesh back."

Tire chains - Chains placed on tires for better traction in snowy conditions.
"We had to use tire chains to get through the snowstorm."
Translation: "We had to put chains on our tires to drive through the snowstorm."

Timbit kid - A young child participating in the Tim Hortons-sponsored minor sports programs.
"He's a proud Timbit kid on his hockey team."
Translation: "He's a proud young child playing on a Tim Hortons-sponsored hockey team."

Timmies double-double - A coffee with two creams and two sugars from Tim Hortons.
"I always get a Timmies double-double in the morning."
Translation: "I always get a coffee with two creams and two sugars from Tim Hortons in the morning."

Tundra buggy - A vehicle designed for traveling over Arctic tundra.
"We took a tundra buggy tour to see the polar bears."
Translation: "We took a tour in a vehicle designed for Arctic terrain to see the polar bears."

True North - A poetic term for Canada, from the national anthem "O Canada."

"We are proud citizens of the True North."
Translation: "We are proud Canadians."

Toque toss - A tradition where fans throw toques onto the ice after a hat trick.
"There was a huge toque toss after his third goal."
Translation: "Fans threw their knit caps onto the ice after his third goal."

Tommy - A slang term for a common soldier, often used during World War I.
"My great-grandfather was a Tommy in the war."
Translation: "My great-grandfather was a common soldier in the war."

Timmy's card - A gift card for Tim Hortons, often given as a small token of appreciation.
"She gave me a Timmy's card for helping out."
Translation: "She gave me a gift card for Tim Hortons as a thank-you."

Tic-tac-toe - A quick passing play in hockey leading to a goal.
"That was a perfect tic-tac-toe play for the win!"
Translation: "That was a perfect quick passing play in hockey that led to a goal and a win!"

Tree line - The edge of the habitat at which trees are capable of growing.
"We hiked all the way to the tree line."
Translation: "We hiked up to the edge of the habitat where trees can grow."

Two-four - A case of 24 beers.
"We picked up a two-four for the party."
Translation: "We bought a case of 24 beers for the party."

Terry Fox Run - An annual charity event in honor of Terry Fox, a Canadian hero who ran across Canada to raise money for cancer research.
"We're participating in the Terry Fox Run this year."
Translation: "We're taking part in the annual charity event to raise money for cancer research."

Timmies roll up the rim - A popular contest at Tim Hortons where customers can win prizes by rolling up the rim of their coffee cup.
"Did you win anything in the Timmies roll up the rim?"
Translation: "Did you win any prizes in the contest at Tim Hortons

U

Ukkusiksalik - A national park in Nunavut, known for its Arctic wildlife and landscapes.
"We spent a week exploring Ukkusiksalik."
Translation: "We spent a week exploring the national park in Nunavut known for its Arctic wildlife."

Under the weather - Feeling unwell or sick.
"I'm feeling a bit under the weather today."
Translation: "I'm feeling a bit sick today."

Up north - Refers to the northern regions of Canada, often implying remote or Arctic areas.
"We're planning a trip up north next summer."
Translation: "We're planning a trip to the northern or remote regions of Canada next summer."

Uptick - A small increase or improvement.
"There's been an uptick in tourism this year."
Translation: "There has been a small increase in tourism this year."

U-Turn - A maneuver in which a vehicle turns around to go in the opposite direction.
"We missed the exit, so we had to make a U-turn."
Translation: "We missed the exit, so we had to turn around to go back."

Uncleared - Refers to snow or obstacles that haven't been removed.
"The road is uncleared, so be careful driving."

Translation: "The road has not been cleared of snow or obstacles, so drive carefully."

Undergrad - Short for undergraduate, referring to a student pursuing their first degree.
"She's an undergrad at the University of Toronto."
Translation: "She's a student pursuing her first degree at the University of Toronto."

Ukrainian Easter - A traditional Easter celebration observed by Ukrainian Canadians.
"We celebrated Ukrainian Easter with traditional foods."
Translation: "We celebrated Easter with traditional foods from Ukrainian culture."

Urban prairie - An urban area in the prairies, such as cities in Alberta or Saskatchewan.
"Calgary is a bustling urban prairie."
Translation: "Calgary is a busy city located in the prairie region of Canada."

Underdog - A person or team expected to lose but who has a chance to win.
"The team was the underdog but managed to win the game."
Translation: "The team was expected to lose but managed to win."

Undercover - Working secretly, often used in law enforcement or investigation.

"The officer went undercover to investigate the crime."

Translation: "The officer worked secretly to investigate the crime."

Uplift - To raise or improve something, often used metaphorically for mood or spirit.
"The community event really uplifted everyone's spirits."
Translation: "The community event greatly improved everyone's mood."

Utility vehicle - A vehicle designed for various uses, including off-road driving.
"We used the utility vehicle to navigate the rough terrain."
Translation: "We used the vehicle designed for various uses to drive on the rough terrain."

Unplugged - Describes a state where electronic devices are turned off or disconnected.
"We spent the weekend unplugged at the cabin."
Translation: "We spent the weekend without electronic devices at the cabin."

Uptake - The process of accepting or beginning to use something new.
"There's been a slow uptake of the new policy."
Translation: "The process of accepting the new policy has been slow."

Urban sprawl - The expansion of urban areas into rural or undeveloped land.
"Urban sprawl is affecting the countryside around Toronto."
Translation: "The expansion of the city is affecting the countryside around Toronto."

Unseasonably - Refers to weather that is unusual for the time of year.
"We had unseasonably warm weather in November."
Translation: "We had weather that was unusually warm for November."

Undercurrent - A hidden or underlying aspect of a situation.
"There was an undercurrent of tension during the meeting."
Translation: "There was a hidden or underlying feeling of tension during the meeting."

Uplands - Higher areas of land, often used in reference to rural or natural regions.
"The hiking trail leads to beautiful uplands."
Translation: "The hiking trail leads to higher areas of land with beautiful views."

V

Vancouverite - A resident of Vancouver, British Columbia.
"The Vancouverite recommended the best sushi place."
Translation: "The resident of Vancouver recommended the best sushi restaurant."

Vermilion - A town in Alberta, known for its agricultural community.
"We drove through Vermilion on our way to Edmonton."
Translation: "We drove through the town in Alberta known for its agriculture on our way to Edmonton."

Valley - A term used to describe a low area between hills or mountains, often used in place names.
"The wine region is located in the valley."
Translation: "The wine region is located in the low area between hills or mountains."

Veto - The power to reject or prohibit something.
"The mayor used his veto power on the new policy."
Translation: "The mayor rejected the new policy using his power."

Vortex - A whirling mass of fluid or air, often used metaphorically.
"The political vortex in Ottawa is heating up."
Translation: "The political situation in Ottawa is becoming more intense."

Vex - To annoy or worry.
"The constant noise vexes me."
Translation: "The continuous noise annoys or worries me."

Vicarious - Experienced through someone else's actions.
"I live vicariously through my friends' travel stories."
Translation: "I experience excitement through my friends' travel stories."

Voyeur - Someone who gains pleasure from observing others, often in secret.
"He felt like a voyeur peeking through the curtains."
Translation: "He felt like someone who secretly observes others, peeking through the curtains."

W

Whiz-bang - Describes something that is impressive or exciting, often with a sense of flashiness.
"The fireworks display was a real whiz-bang event."
Translation: "The fireworks show was very impressive and exciting."

Wicked - Used to describe something that is great or impressive.
"That was a wicked performance!"
Translation: "That was an impressive performance!"

Wolverine - A large, fierce mammal native to northern Canada, also used as a mascot for the University of Michigan.
"We spotted a wolverine in the wild during our hike."
Translation: "We saw a large, fierce mammal in the wild during our hike."

Wristy - A term used in hockey to describe a shot taken with a quick flick of the wrist.
"He scored with a wristy shot from the blue line."
Translation: "He scored with a quick flick of the wrist in hockey from the blue line."

Waffle - To speak or write evasively or indecisively.
"Stop waffling and make a decision!"
Translation: "Stop being indecisive and make a decision!"

Wack - Slang for something that is strange or off, sometimes used to describe something of poor quality.
"That movie was totally wack."
Translation: "That movie was strange or of poor quality."

Whippersnapper - An energetic or young person, sometimes with a connotation of being inexperienced.
"That young whippersnapper has a lot of talent."
Translation: "That energetic young person has a lot of talent."

Wilderness - Untamed natural areas, often used to describe remote and wild places in Canada.
"We spent the weekend exploring the Canadian wilderness."
Translation: "We spent the weekend exploring the untamed natural areas in Canada."

Wheeler-dealer - Someone who is skilled at making deals or transactions, often in a business context.
"He's a real wheeler-dealer in the business world."
Translation: "He's very skilled at making deals in business."

Warm-up - A period of exercise or preparation before a more strenuous activity.
"We did a quick warm-up before the game."
Translation: "We performed some light exercise before the game."

Wasteland - An area that is barren or desolate, often used to describe neglected or degraded areas.
"The abandoned factory site was a real wasteland."

Translation: "The neglected site of the abandoned factory was barren and desolate."

Woo - To try to gain the favor of someone, often in a romantic context.
"He tried to woo her with flowers and chocolates."
Translation: "He tried to gain her favor with flowers and chocolates."

Wanderlust - A strong desire to travel and explore the world.
"Her wanderlust took her to many countries."
Translation: "Her strong desire to travel led her to many countries."

Wrap - To finish or conclude something.
"Let's wrap up the meeting."
Translation: "Let's conclude the meeting."

Wrestle - To engage in physical combat or struggle, often used metaphorically.
"He had to wrestle with his decision to move."
Translation: "He had to struggle with making the decision to move."

Whirlwind - A rapidly rotating column of air or a situation that is chaotic and fast-moving.
"The week was a whirlwind of activity."
Translation: "The week was a chaotic and fast-moving series of events."

Windchill - The effect of wind that makes the temperature feel colder than it actually is.

"The windchill made it feel like -30°C outside."
Translation: "The wind made the temperature feel much colder than it actually was."

Wigwam - A type of Native American dwelling, often used in the context of Indigenous culture in Canada.
"We stayed in a traditional wigwam during our visit."
Translation: "We stayed in a traditional Indigenous dwelling during our visit."

Wok - A type of pan used in Asian cooking, commonly found in Canadian kitchens with diverse cuisines.
"We used the wok to stir-fry the vegetables."
Translation: "We used the pan to quickly cook the vegetables."

Whiz - To move quickly or with great speed.
"The car whizzed by on the highway."
Translation: "The car moved quickly along the highway."

Y

Yankee - A term historically used to refer to Americans, sometimes used playfully in Canada.
"He's always joking about being a Yankee."
Translation: "He often makes playful references to being American."

Yukon - A territory in Canada known for its natural beauty and wilderness.
"We're going to explore the Yukon next summer."
Translation: "We plan to visit the Canadian territory known for its natural beauty next summer."

Yodel - A type of singing that involves rapid changes in pitch.
"She performed a yodeling song at the festival."
Translation: "She sang a song with rapid changes in pitch at the festival."

Yawn - To open the mouth wide and inhale deeply, often due to tiredness.
"I couldn't stop yawning during the long meeting."
Translation: "I kept opening my mouth wide and inhaling deeply due to tiredness during the meeting."

Yarn - A type of thread used for knitting or weaving, also used to refer to a long, often exaggerated story.
"She told us a yarn about her adventure in the Rockies."
Translation: "She shared a long, possibly exaggerated story about her adventure."

Yew - A type of evergreen tree with red berries, often used in landscaping.
"The yew trees in the garden add a touch of green all year."
Translation: "The evergreen trees in the garden provide year-round greenery."

Yoke - A wooden beam used to join two animals together for work, or a metaphor for a burden.
"The oxen wore a yoke for plowing the fields."
Translation: "The animals wore a wooden beam to help them work together in the fields."

Yippee - An exclamation of excitement or joy.
"The kids shouted 'yippee' when they saw the snow."
Translation: "The kids expressed excitement with a joyful exclamation upon seeing the snow."

Yuppie - A term used to describe a young urban professional, often with connotations of affluence.
"The neighborhood has a lot of yuppies moving in."
Translation: "The area has many young, affluent professionals moving in."

Yowza - An exclamation of surprise or excitement.
"Yowza! That's an impressive collection."
Translation: "Wow! That's a very impressive collection."

Yellowknife - The capital city of the Northwest Territories, known for its beautiful northern lights.
"We saw the northern lights while in Yellowknife."
Translation: "We observed the aurora borealis while visiting the capital city of the Northwest Territories."

Yammer - To talk continuously and often annoyingly.
"He kept yammering about his vacation."
Translation: "He continued talking on and on about his vacation, often annoyingly."

Yield - To produce or provide something, often used in reference to crops or results.
"The farm yielded a good crop this year."
Translation: "The farm produced a good harvest this year."

Yearn - To have a strong desire or longing for something.
"She yearned for the tranquility of the countryside."
Translation: "She had a strong desire for the peacefulness of the rural area."

Yank - To pull something suddenly or sharply.
"He gave the rope a yank to see if it would move."
Translation: "He pulled the rope suddenly to check if it would move."

Yelp - A short, sharp cry or bark, often from an animal.
"The dog let out a yelp when it hurt its paw."
Translation: "The dog made a short, sharp sound when it injured its paw."

Yeoman - A person who performs practical or agricultural work, historically used to describe a free man holding a small estate.
"The yeoman took care of the farm and its duties."
Translation: "The person who worked on and managed the small estate took care of farm duties."

Yule - An old term for Christmas or the Christmas season. "We celebrated Yule with festive decorations."
Translation: "We celebrated Christmas with festive decorations."

Z

Zenith - The highest point or peak of something.
"The project reached its zenith last year."
Translation: "The project reached its highest point last year."

Zipline - A cable or wire used to slide from one point to another, often used in adventure activities.
"We went ziplining through the forest canopy."
Translation: "We used a cable to slide through the forest canopy for adventure."

Zest - Enthusiasm or excitement, also the outer peel of citrus fruits used for flavor.
"She approached the project with great zest."
Translation: "She tackled the project with a lot of enthusiasm."

Zinc - A chemical element used in various applications, including galvanizing and batteries.
"The batteries contain zinc."
Translation: "The batteries use the chemical element zinc."

Zany - Amusingly unconventional or eccentric.
"The comedian's zany antics kept us laughing all night."
Translation: "The comedian's unconventional and eccentric actions made us laugh."

Zephyr - A gentle, mild breeze.
"A soft zephyr blew through the open window."
Translation: "A gentle breeze flowed through the open window."

Zestful - Full of energy and enthusiasm.
"Her zestful attitude brightens up the room."
Translation: "Her energetic and enthusiastic attitude makes the room brighter."

Zygote - The cell formed by the union of sperm and egg, marking the start of development.
"The zygote begins to divide and develop into an embryo."
Translation: "The cell formed from sperm and egg starts dividing and developing into an embryo."

Manufactured by Amazon.ca
Bolton, ON